Molly Brown's Capitol Hill Neighborhood

LEIGH A. GRINSTEAD

PHOTOGRAPHY BY
CYNTHIA S. HERRICK

HISTORIC DENVER, INC.

D0912308

To Seth and Emma, for inspiring me to get up and do my best each and every day. Thank you.

This project was partially funded by a State Historical Fund grant award from the Colorado Historical Society, and with the assistance of Historic Denver, Inc. Historic Denver thanks the Vance Kirkland Museum and Foundation for their contribution to and generous support of this publication.

International Standard Book Number: 0-914248-17-0
Text copyright © 1997, 2002 second edition Leigh A. Grinstead
Photographs copyright © 1997, 2002 Cynthia S. Herrick
unless otherwise noted

Cover photo: Sheedy Mansion, 1115–1121 Grant Street

All rights reserved.
Published by
Historic Denver, Inc.
1536 Wynkoop Street, Suite 400A
Denver, Colorado 80202-1182

Printed by Crossfire Graphics.

Editor: Lori D. Kranz
Proofreaders: Robin Cerwonka and Cyndie Chandler
Indexers: Caryl Riedel and Cyndie Chandler
Design and Composition: Cathy Calder, Blonde Ambition

CONTENTS

ST. GEORGE AND THE DRAGON
ADORN THE BIDDLE REEVES HOUSE
AT 1459 PENNSYLVANIA.

ACKNOWLEDGMENTS

I would like to thank Gheda Gayou, Gail Silber, and Nancy L. Widmann for their research and information; Cathy Calder for her design skills; and Phil Goodstein, Hugh Grant, Peg Ekstrand, Steve Grinstead, David Halaas, Amber Kawczak, Tasha McDonald, Tom Noel, Annette Vanasse, and Holly Victor for their interest, time, and very helpful comments. I also thank Kathleen Brooker, president of Historic Denver, Inc., Kim Grant, and Kris Christensen for their help and support over time while I wrote, and then rewrote, portions of this guide. Thanks to the staff at the Molly Brown House Museum for holding down the fort when I was revising the manuscript: Kerri Atter, Monica Dean, Andrea Dvorkin, Anne Hogan, Heidi Trevithick, and Elizabeth Walker.

The authors of the other three volumes in the initial series—Nancy Widmann, Jack Murphy, and Diane Wilk—all contributed in various ways to the creation of the original book, and I appreciate their invaluable feedback as much now as I did in 1997. I am indebted to Hugh Grant and the Vance Kirkland Museum and Foundation, who felt this project was worthy of revision and financial support—thank you for the push! Finally, I thank Lori Kranz for her continued good humor, patience, and skill in editing this book. It is always a pleasure.

THE ROOFLINE
OF THE NEO-JACOBEAN
JOHN PORTER HOUSE

INTRODUCTION

This project began in 1994 in response to the many requests received from Molly Brown House visitors for information about other historic homes in the Capitol Hill area. For years I have walked through Molly's neighborhood and wondered about these beautiful old homes and the people who once lived in them.

In early 1995, Historic Denver, Inc., published what I consider to be the first version of this book, *Molly Brown's Capitol Hill Walking Tour*. I was pleased with and proud of that edition, but when the first book in the Historic Denver Guides series was produced in late 1995, it became apparent that the original walking tour could be adapted to the newer format with more detailed photographs and a different emphasis. The opportunity to rework the earlier version allowed me to gain a new perspective on the material and add an architectural emphasis. I also spent time collecting new information about the people who lived in Molly Brown's neighborhood. For example, many people who lived in Capitol Hill had strong connections to the Catholic Church and were instrumental in building the Cathedral of the Immaculate Conception, and many of the occupants of the structures that comprise these tours were mining and railroad magnates. There were others, some that I missed in 1997. When the opportunity arose to revise the text and add sites, I jumped at the chance. I hope that the guide will continue to provide answers to the curious, as well as introduce newcomers to the architecture and history of Denver's Capitol Hill. In many ways the result is a thumbnail sketch of the architects and people who shaped early Denver.

These tours are not necessarily intended to be walked in a single day, although it can be done. Rather, they are a way to sample and enjoy the history of various Capitol Hill neighborhoods, areas you may end up visiting over and over again. It is impossible to estimate the length of time a complete tour of all sixty-two structures would take; it depends on whether you take a brisk walk or linger over each house on your favorite block.

Sites marked **N⊞R** are listed in the National Register of Historic Places and those marked **D⊞L** have been designated Denver Landmarks. Information on the historic names of the buildings, when the structures were built, their architectural styles, their owners and occupants through the years, the architects who designed them, and the cost of the building, if known, is also included. I welcome any additional information, interesting tidbits, or comments you may have. At the end of this guide is a list of sources I found helpful in the search for information about these homes and their many residents. I also relied heavily on information found in Denver Landmark applications at the Denver City and County Building, and in the National Register of Historic Places forms at the Colorado Historical Society.

History

Arriving in Denver in 1860, H. C. Brown and John W. Smith were the men primarily responsible for the development of Capitol Hill. In 1862, Congress passed the Homestead Act, which gave ownership of up to 160 acres of public land to individuals who resided on and cultivated it for five years after their initial claim. Brown used the act to lay claim to the area bounded by what is now 11th and 20th Avenues, and the half block west of Broadway to the alley between Grant and Logan Streets. He built a cabin at 12th and Sherman and held on to his property, believing that Denver would expand and eventually build on "Brown's Bluff." Brown laid out the east-west and north-south grid of Capitol Hill's streets. Denver had been platting streets and avenues on a diagonal grid to follow the course of water in lower downtown. In 1867, Governor A. Cameron Hunt proclaimed that the territory would build a capitol if someone would donate ten acres for the site. Brown responded and immediately donated the area from Lincoln to Grant Streets and from Colfax to 14th Avenues. He wasn't the only donor, however. Twelve other sites were donated as well.

Capitol Hill was dusty and seen as virtually useless land until John W. Smith brought water to the area. Smith homesteaded from Colfax to 13th and from the Grant/Logan alley east to Clarkson Street. In 1864, he was hired to construct a 25-mile ditch that would take water from the Platte River up to Capitol Hill. The project, which became known as the "big ditch," was the largest factor in the residential and agricultural growth on the Hill. Throughout the nineteenth century, the ditch was changed and adapted to bring water to the expanding population. The ditch was completed in 1867, and by the 1870s the first mansions began to appear on Capitol Hill.

FREDERICK STERNER'S GEORGIAN REVIVAL AT 950 LOGAN (CAMPBELL MANSION)

Away from the pollution, rush, noise, gambling dens, and the even seedier places of downtown, the area known as Capitol Hill gave the privileged a grand view of the Rockies. In the 1880s the lucky few who made their millions from the mountains, the railroads, or trade quickly moved up onto the Hill to display their newfound wealth for the multitudes to see. By 1892, Denver experienced a building and real estate boom. Silver king Horace W. Tabor, H. C. Brown (owner and builder of the Brown Palace), millionaire Dennis Sheedy, philanthropist J. K. Mullen, and others bought prime lots and hired such well-known architects as William Lang, Frank Edbrooke, Fisher and Fisher, and Varian and Sterner to design beautiful and elaborate homes. They favored the architectural styles of the day: the now classic Queen Anne, the elaborate and eclectic Richardsonian Romanesque, the refined Neoclassical.

But the boom couldn't last—the economic Panic of 1893 hit hard. Although it was a nationwide depression, Denver was especially affected. The federal government came up with many solutions, one of which was to repeal the Sherman Silver Purchase Act. Under this act, the government bought up silver to use as the backing for U.S. currency; the repeal of the act changed the money standard to gold. In Colorado, silver mining was the leading industry.

As Tom Noel and Barbara Norgren write in *Denver: The City Beautiful*, "Half of the city's banks failed in 1893, and thousands of properties were sold to anyone able to pay delinquent taxes. More than half of the 600 realtors listed in the 1893 city directory were out of business two years later. Ambitious plans for new downtown buildings and for suburban residential neighborhoods were mothballed. While 2,338 building permits had been granted in 1890, only 124 permits were issued in Denver in 1894."

Capitol Hill began to change. Upper-middle-class houses went up alongside the older mansions. Apartment buildings and more modest houses for servants and the working classes were built as well. In the 1920s a wave of apartment buildings were built. In the 1930s, with the onset of the Great Depression, it became rare to find single-family, owner-occupied houses. Almost everyone took in renters. In the 1950s and 1960s, Denver suffered from urban renewal: Many of its finest buildings were bulldozed, residential apartment towers completely out of scale with the neighborhood were erected, and houses were demolished to create parking lots. In 1967 the city established the Denver Landmark Preservation Commission, which helps residents and businesses restore and preserve their historic properties. It also allows neighborhoods like Capitol Hill to establish historic districts so that the history of an area can be maintained and future development will conform to community standards. In 1970, Historic Denver, Inc., was founded to preserve the Molly Brown House Museum. Historic Denver is a private, nonprofit organization dedicated to the preservation of Denver's built environment. New, historically sensitive development is occurring in historic structures, and clean, street-friendly businesses are opening up. The twenty-first century will inevitably bring new challenges to Capitol Hill, but in its diversity, there is strength.

This Neoclassical central arch support fronts the Foursquare Taylor House.

TOUR ONE

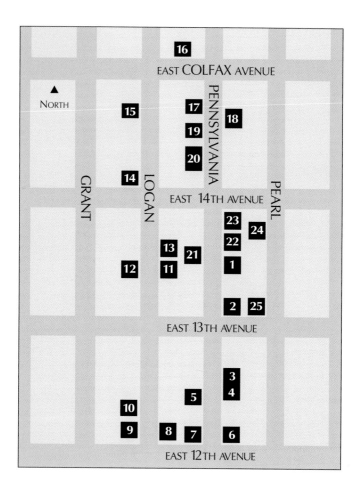

KEY

1

MOLLY BROWN HOUSE

1340 PENNSYLVANIA STREET

Architectural style: QUEEN ANNE

Built: 1889

Architect: WILLIAM LANG

This house was built in 1889 for Isaac and Mary Large, who sold it to J. J. Brown in 1893 or 1894 for $30,000. Brown had worked his way west through jobs in various mining camps. As a superintendent for the Ibex Mining Company in Leadville (owned by John F. Campion), he oversaw the Little Jonny Mine, which in 1894 produced one of the widest veins of gold and high-grade copper ore ever found. J. J. and his wife, Margaret "Molly" Tobin Brown, moved into the house in April 1894. Because of J. J.'s subsequent ill health, the result of his many years spent in the mines, the deed was transferred into Molly's name in 1902. Molly, who achieved international recognition as the heroine of the 1912 *Titanic* disaster, owned the home until her death in 1932, after which the house and its contents were sold at auction. Following a succession of five owners over the next forty years, Historic Denver bought the house in 1970 for $80,000 and opened it as a museum. Since then, Historic Denver has spent approximately $1 million on its restoration.

The work of prominent Denver architect William Lang is characterized by an eclectic mix of architectural styles, apparent in this combination of a Queen Anne structure with Romanesque Revival touches such as rusticated stonework and arches. Lang's exuberant style is continued throughout the house with four decorative fireplaces, three stained-glass windows, a painted conservatory ceiling in the dining room, and a combination of golden oak, cherry, and mahogany woodwork on the first floor. For information on building materials, see *Geology Tour of Denver's Capitol Hill Stone Buildings*, part of this series.

It is unknown where Lang was trained, but between 1888 and 1893 he designed more than 150 houses in Denver. The 1893 depression ruined his thriving career. He remained in Denver for the next two years, even though new construction had come to a virtual standstill. By 1895, Lang was in severe financial difficulty, poor health, and suffering from progressive dementia brought on by depression. He left Denver in 1896 to spend time with a brother in Chicago. His life ended when he was hit by a train in August 1897.

KNOWN AS THE HOUSE OF LIONS
DURING ITS BOARDINGHOUSE DAYS

PHOTO: © 1997 KEN E. ERICKSON

2

PENN GARAGE
1300 PENNSYLVANIA STREET

Architectural style: TWENTIETH-CENTURY COMMERCIAL

Built: 1924

Architect: UNKNOWN

In Capitol Hill, structures such as the Penn Garage were built to house automobiles when recreational cars began to replace the horse and carriage. Wealthier families in the neighborhood stored their automobiles at the Penn Garage, including Molly Brown, who kept her Fritchle 100-mile Electric here.

This vehicle was one of the most expensive and elaborate cars of its day. Oliver Fritchle opened his electric car company in Denver in 1904, and by 1910 moved the factory to the building now known as Mammoth Gardens, at Colfax and Clarkson. The company hand made probably no more than 500 cars. It produced its own axles, steering parts, motors, controllers, and batteries, and even had its own sewing department. Its employees were recruited from old carriage manufacturing companies.

In 1914, the Fritchle 100-mile Electric was selling for $1,500 to $2,000; a Ford Runabout cost only $400. The cars had inlaid wood and fine upholstery, crystal dome lights that came on when a door opened, and even a crystal bud vase. The voluminous interior could accommodate the hats and fashions of the day.

According to Cecelia Burkhardt, whose grandparents owned the Adolf Roedere Bakery at 10th and Larimer, where Molly Brown often enjoyed a cup of coffee, Mrs. Roedere often remarked, "Just think, to see such a vehicle where there was horse and wagon before, and to see a woman driving it!"

The 1917 invention of the self-starter for gas engines signaled the decline of electric automobiles such as the Fritchle. Today one can see quite possibly the last surviving example of a Denver-manufactured automobile, and an example of what Molly Brown's car looked like, at the Colorado History Museum.

The Penn Garage has remained a Capitol Hill landmark and serviced automobiles for more than seventy years. In early 1997, it was purchased and renovated into lofts. Other commercial garages throughout Capitol Hill were built in a similar style and have the same red and blond brick and window patterns.

Simple brickwork characteristic of early Twentieth-Century Commercial buildings

3 # FREDERICK HOUSE
1258 PENNSYLVANIA STREET

Architectural style:
FOURSQUARE

Built:
1884–88

Architect:
UNKNOWN

1258 Pennsylvania was built by John Frederick between 1884 and 1888. Frederick, who ran a successful printing shop on Larimer Street in downtown Denver, lived here while the house next door was being constructed. Perhaps he built the first house for sale, because when 1254 Pennsylvania was finished in 1893, he immediately moved in.

4 # FREDERICK HOUSE
1254 PENNSYLVANIA STREET

Architectural style: QUEEN ANNE

Built: 1893

Architect: UNKNOWN

1254 and 1258 Pennsylvania may appear to be on very small lots, but narrow lots were quite common at the time. Notice that the two houses actually touch. Both houses feature detailed wooden trim, and the sandstone wreath motifs of the first-floor window surrounds of 1254 Pennsylvania are echoed elsewhere on both houses.

1 2 5 8 P ENNSYLVANIA
WINDOW DETAIL

ROBINSON HOUSE

1225 PENNSYLVANIA STREET

Architectural style: CRAFTSMAN

Built: 1906

Architects: MAREAN AND NORTON

The Robinson House, considered the height of fashion in its day, is a Craftsman-style home. It is much more streamlined than most Victorian houses of the period. It is distinguished by a low-pitched gabled roof, wide overhanging eaves, and exposed roof rafters.

Willis Marean was one of Denver's most active architects. A New Yorker, Marean settled in Denver in 1880 and worked for the Edbrooke firm until 1895, when he and Albert Norton formed a partnership. The work was slow until after 1900, when Marean and Norton designed buildings such as the Governor's Mansion (see *Geology Tour of Denver's Capitol Hill Stone Buildings*), the YMCA building at 16th and Lincoln, the Decker Branch Library, the Greek theater and colonnade in Civic Center Park, and the pavilion in Cheesman Park.

Their client on this project, Mary Byers Robinson, was the daughter of William Byers, owner of the *Rocky Mountain News*. Her husband, W. F. Robinson, worked at the paper before their marriage in 1879. He then managed the *Leadville Democrat* for two years before founding the W. F. Robinson Printing Company, which he operated until his death in 1912. Mary continued to live in the house until 1929. An accomplished photographer and pianist, she traveled widely and remained socially active throughout her life. She died in 1940 after an automobile accident.

A MIX OF BLOND BRICK, DARK WOOD, AND STUCCO
EMPHASIZE THE ARCHITECTURE.

DUNNING-BENEDICT RESIDENCE NOR DOL
1200 PENNSYLVANIA STREET

Architectural style: RICHARDSONIAN ROMANESQUE
Built: 1889
Architect: WILLIAM LANG

This stunning gray stone mansion still displays the original stained-glass window with its prominent peacock. Note the beautiful and intricate carved stonework of this stately yet eclectic home.

Henry Hobson Richardson was one of the most influential architects of the nineteenth century. He single-handedly created a revival of the Romanesque style, with its symmetrical facades, round-topped arches over windows, and rusticated masonry. Prominent Denver architect William Lang designed this home in 1889 for Walter Dunning.

Dunning, born in Mount Ayr, Iowa, served with the Iowa Infantry in the Civil War and was discharged in 1865. He married Jane Elizabeth Fellows, and after several years of marriage, they moved with their three children to Denver, where Dunning became a real estate developer.

The Dunnings sold the house in 1898 to Mitchell Benedict, also a Civil War veteran, who had moved to Denver from New York after the war. The politically active lawyer lived here with his wife, Mary Caroline Doolittle-Benedict, and their son, James. Mitchell died in 1906.

In 1903, Walter Cheesman moved into this house. In 1906 his health failed, and he died in 1907. The Benedict family owned the gray stone house until 1930, after which it changed ownership many times. Like many Capitol Hill mansions, it served diverse purposes—hotel, apartment building, offices, and convalescent home—before being lovingly restored. Currently it houses law offices on the first floor and a few spacious apartments on the second and third floors as well as in the carriage house.

William Lang was undoubtedly Denver's greatest eclectic architect of the nineteenth century, practicing here from 1887 to 1895. Lang designed both commercial and domestic structures, but the bulk of his work focused on brick and stone residences in an eclectic combination of Romanesque and Queen Anne styles. For information on this home's building materials, see *Geology Tour of Denver's Capitol Hill Stone Buildings*, part of this series.

LEAVING NO SURFACE UNCARVED,
THE STONEMASON "SOFTENED"
THE MANSION.

KEATING MANSION

1207 PENNSYLVANIA STREET

Architectural style: QUEEN ANNE/ROMANESQUE REVIVAL

Built: 1891

Architects: REICHE, CARTER AND SMITH

Sharing many elements of the Dunning-Benedict Residence (stop 6), yet of a different character and materials, is the Capitol Hill Mansion Bed and Breakfast, also known as the Keating Mansion. This mansion, with its rough masonry walls, was built for Jeffrey and Mary Keating in 1891. Mansions like this were going up everywhere in Capitol Hill between 1891 and 1894. Completed before the Silver Crash of 1893, the Keating Mansion exemplifies the exuberance of the era.

Jeffrey Keating was a prominent businessman with ventures in real estate, insurance, and the McPhee & McGinnity Lumber Company. (The lumber company was a large supporter of the building of the Cathedral of the Immaculate Conception, cutting costs to assist the parish during construction.) Mary Keating was very active in social affairs and gave much of her time to charity events. After the Keatings moved to York Street in 1900, they rented their house to Charles Bayly, owner of the Underhill Manufacturing Company of Denver. In 1902 they sold the house for $30,000 to powerful industrialist John W. Nesmith.

A self-made millionaire, Nesmith began life as a mechanic and managed, through self-education and hard work, to become one of the foremost authorities on mining and smelting. He resided in the house until his wife, Elizabeth, died in 1910. The house passed to the two Nesmith daughters in 1914, who kept it in the family until 1923, and then sold it to the Crew family for $20,000. The Crews lived in the house for a year before turning it into the Buena Vista Hotel.

The house changed hands often, serving as an apartment building, a convalescent home, and an office. In 1993 it was renovated and opened as the Capitol Hill Mansion Bed and Breakfast. Because much of the original plasterwork, woodwork, and windows was intact, the renovation consisted mainly of removing walls and doorways to restore the original floor plan. For information on the building materials, see *Geology Tour of Denver's Capitol Hill Stone Buildings*, part of this series.

THE TURRET OF 1207 PENNSYLVANIA

BAKER HOUSE

D⬛L

1208 LOGAN STREET

Architectural style: COTTAGE

Built: 1886

Architect: UNKNOWN

This charming cottage with its white picket fence was built in 1886 and is probably the last wooden frame house built on Capitol Hill. After several large and destructive fires in the 1870s and 1880s, city building codes required that houses be built with brick frames. Notable features of the all-wooden house include fish-scale shingling on the second story and a decorative bracket on the south side below the mullioned window.

Anna and Henry P. Baker built the house for themselves. Henry was a collector and timekeeper for the Colorado Telephone Company. Later he became timekeeper for Western Electric. The current resident, Dolores N. Plested, a journalist for the *Trinidad Chronicle* and the *New York Times*, is a member of the Denver Woman's Press Club up the street (stop 12).

A RARE WOOD-FRAMED REMNANT FROM DAYS WHEN
DESTRUCTIVE FIRES RAVAGED DENVER

RAYMOND HOUSE
1209 LOGAN STREET

Architectural style: QUEEN ANNE

Built: 1884

Architect: UNKNOWN

The Raymond House is a classic Queen Anne with decorative brick-work. It was built in 1884 for Charles Raymond as a speculative venture. He owned much of Logan Street, called Kansas Street at the time, and sold this house to Joseph Davis in 1887. Davis, a realtor, lived in the house until 1897, when he sold it to James Reynolds and his wife, Madge Smiley, sister of Denver historian Jerome Smiley.

Madge was known as the "Friend of the Friendless" for her tireless crusading for the downtrodden. She was a well-known poet and active in most early twentieth-century charity campaigns. The Reynoldses lived modestly in this cottage, although they had the means to be part of Capitol Hill high society. Madge preferred to use her wealth to provide for the poor. Her closest male friends were longtime rivals Thomas Patterson, owner of the *Rocky Mountain News*, who lived in the Chateauesque mansion at 11th and Pennsylvania, and Frederick Bonfils, owner of the *Denver Post*, who lived on the southeast corner of 10th and Humboldt. Madge and Bonfils grew extremely close, and he publicly referred to her as "Dearest." On February 21, 1908, after horseback riding with Bonfils, Madge died suddenly. Bonfils was reported to have fainted and gone into shock when he learned of her death. Patterson was a pall-bearer at her funeral.

HOME OF MADGE REYNOLDS,
"FRIEND OF THE FRIENDLESS"

ARDELT'S
1225 LOGAN STREET

Architectural style: QUEEN ANNE

Built: 1884

Architect: UNKNOWN

Ardelt's Flowers now occupies the home and florist shop built for Edward and Rosalie Mauff in 1884. Edward was a shoemaker who owned a shop on Larimer Street. Rosalie started her floral business with a single hothouse where she grew geraniums, the ever-popular Victorian flower. By 1910, Mauff's was the largest greenhouse in the West, with the hothouses extending north almost to the corner of 13th Avenue. Molly Brown and other Denver residents bought their flowers here.

Over the years, the building has remained essentially the same—with a florist shop (now a gift shop) downstairs and the upper floors used as a residence.

ARDELT'S ECLECTIC ROOFLINE

RHOADS HOUSE
1330 LOGAN STREET

Architectural style: DENVER SQUARE

Built: 1898

Architect: UNKNOWN

Between Ardelt's and 1330 Logan Street are apartment buildings in a variety of architectural styles typical of Capitol Hill: Art Deco, Tudor, and International.

This classic Denver Square structure sports several subtle decorative features; note the brickwork on the corners and the wooden dentils under the eaves. The false shutters add an open quality to the house. The Rhoads House was built in 1898 for Harry and Addie Rhoads, their son, Harry, and daughter, Hazel. Harry M. Rhoads became a well-known and well-loved photojournalist famous for his images of turn-of-the-century Denver, taken first for the *Denver Republican* and then for the *Rocky Mountain News*. Many of these classic images can be found in the book dedicated to Rhoads's career, *Denver's Man with a Camera*. Hazel Rhoads married Charles Gates, Jr., head of the Gates Rubber Company.

HARRY M. RHOADS, "DENVER'S MAN WITH A CAMERA," LIVED AT THIS SIMPLE FOURSQUARE-INSPIRED RESIDENCE.

DENVER WOMAN'S PRESS CLUB DⓈL
1325 LOGAN STREET

Architectural style: ENGLISH COTTAGE
Built: 1910
Architects: VARIAN AND VARIAN

Currently home to the Denver Woman's Press Club, this house was built in 1910 for artist George Burr as both a residence and a studio. It is a quaint example of the English Cottage style. The low-ceilinged entry has an open staircase that leads to a balcony overlooking the studio, which has north skylights and a vaulted ceiling. The large north window provided Burr with ample light as he worked in his studio.

Burr, who came to Denver in 1906, was a pioneer artist well known for his nature etchings and watercolors; his work is in the collections of the Denver Art Museum, Colorado Historical Society, Denver Public Library, and Boston's Museum of Fine Arts. Because of failing health, he moved to Phoenix, where he died in 1939.

Upon his move in 1924, Burr sold the house to the Denver Woman's Press Club, which was chartered on March 18, 1898, with nineteen members—five female journalists and fourteen society women. The organization was founded to help host a national convention of the General Federation of Woman's Clubs. The Woman's Press Club has sponsored scholarships for promising women students, conducted writing classes and competitions, and hosted such writers as William Faulkner, Robert Frost, and H. G. Wells. Molly Brown was one of the club's early members—she and other wealthy patrons were recruited to help boost membership. As membership grew, the club raised money through balls and luncheons until it was able to purchase the house in 1924.

AN EARLY MEMBER, MOLLY BROWN
HELPED RAISE FUNDS FOR THE NEW
DENVER WOMAN'S PRESS CLUB.

CUTHBERT-DINES HOUSE

D⬛L

1350 LOGAN STREET

Architectural style: GEORGIAN REVIVAL

Built: 1901

Architect: FREDERICK STERNER

Frederick Sterner designed this distinguished, large brick home with quoins, and voussoirs over the second-floor windows. The one-story solarium on the south side provides light, and above the solarium, on the third floor, is a small Palladian window. The first-floor bay windows are luxurious in scale. The entry is truly elegant; the door is flanked by one-story Ionic columns and sidelight panels with leaded glass, surrounded by a carved wooden arch. An elaborate wrought-iron railing flanks the marble stairs. A garage was added in the 1940s; before then, the Dineses stored their carriages and cars at the Penn Garage, just one block east.

Lucius Montrose Cuthbert and his wife, Gertrude Hill Berger Cuthbert, built the house in 1901. Gertrude—the daughter of Nathaniel Hill, owner of the Argo Smelter, publisher of the *Denver Republican*, and U.S. senator from 1879 to 1885—had attended private schools, toured Europe, met royalty, and made her formal debut in Washington, D.C. She married Charles Berger, who died within a few months of their marriage; they had one daughter. The thirty-one-year-old widow married Lucius at St. John's Cathedral in 1900. Lucius was a lawyer who primarily represented English and oil industry clients until his retirement in 1908. This house was a social center, and the Cuthberts were a popular couple.

Lucius died in 1915; his family stayed on until 1923, when they sold the house to Isabel A. and Tyson M. Dines, also an attorney, who specialized in mining and railroad law. He died in 1965. Son Allen followed the family legal tradition. In 1966, he and his wife, Audry, moved into the house, which again became a social center as well as the scene of many Democratic Party and legislative meetings. In 1974, Dines retired from political life and returned to private practice. Twenty years later, he sold the house to Mary Starkey for her Starkey International Institute for Household Management, a school for maids and butlers.

A CAPITOL HILL SOCIAL CENTER
FOR DECADES

FIRST CHURCH OF CHRIST, SCIENTIST   D■L
14TH AVENUE AND LOGAN STREET

Architectural style: NEOCLASSICAL
Built: 1906
Architect: FREDERICK STERNER
Cost: $163,000

On the corner of Logan Street and 14th Avenue is the elegant and impressive First Church of Christ, Scientist. This church, another of Frederick Sterner's designs, is a twentieth-century Neoclassical building with prominent Ionic detailing. It was built in 1906, after the original church at 1751 Logan became too small for its growing congregation. The new church was Capitol Hill's first large structure built of lava rock, and cost $163,000. Inside, the auditorium floor is sloped, and the seating is designed in the fashion of an amphitheater.

DETAILS OF THE FIRST CHURCH
OF CHRIST, SCIENTIST

LOGAN COURT
1461 LOGAN STREET

Architectural style: LIGHT COURT
Built: 1908
Architects: MAREAN AND NORTON

This unassuming apartment building was built in 1908 in the typical Light Court configuration—a U-shaped structure open at the center to allow light to enter each apartment. It was designed by Marean and Norton, who also designed the Governor's Mansion and the Cheesman Memorial (see *Geology Tour of Denver's Capitol Hill Stone Buildings*). Throughout Capitol Hill, architects were creating architecturally interesting and pleasant apartment buildings like this one to attract middle-class residents to the area.

According to Denver historian Phil Goodstein, at the turn of the century, high-quality apartment buildings were being built all over Capitol Hill. These apartments were well constructed, had all the latest amenities, and featured courtyards that filled apartments with light and air. Middle-class tenants flocked to the new buildings and made these apartments home through most of the twentieth century.

Many of Denver's elite were offended that middle-class residents were invading Capitol Hill. In the 1890s, a Pennsylvania, Grant, or Colfax address was a sign of wealth and privilege. With the building of apartments along the same streets, many of the city's wealthy residents started to abandon Capitol Hill proper.

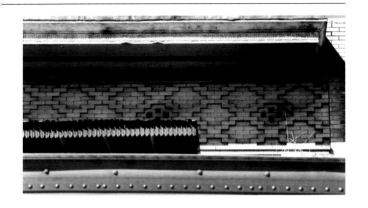

MAREAN AND NORTON PRODUCED MANSIONS AS WELL AS
APARTMENT BUILDINGS.

CATHEDRAL OF THE IMMACULATE CONCEPTION

COLFAX AVENUE AND LOGAN STREET

Architectural style: LATE GOTHIC REVIVAL (FRENCH)

Built: 1902–12

Architects: LEON COQUARD; AARON M. GOVE AND THOMAS F. WALSH

Cost: $500,000

The twin spires of the Cathedral of the Immaculate Conception rise above the northeast corner of Colfax and Logan. Four wealthy and prominent members of the parish—J. J. Brown, John F. Campion, J. K. Mullen, and Dennis Sheedy—paid $28,000 for the future site of the cathedral. A groundbreaking ceremony was held in 1902 and a cornerstone was placed on July 15, 1906.

The cathedral's design was begun in 1900 by Leon Coquard of Detroit, who was forced to retire from the project because of illness. It was finished by Denver's Gove and Walsh, whose work includes Denver's Union Station. In 1912 the cathedral featured the latest technology: telephones, fireproof steel frame construction, tungsten lighting, and an up-to-date ventilation system. Campion's family donated the fifteen bells. When the cathedral was finally dedicated on October 27, 1912, 20,000 people paraded up Colfax to celebrate.

Denver's high society attended the 11:00 A.M. Sunday Mass, known as one of the best fashion shows in town. According to historian Tom Noel, ushers wore morning coats, pin-striped trousers, and white gloves as they unhooked the purple velvet drapes for parishioners who "owned" purple-pillowed pews. Pews cost 25 cents for adults and 10 cents for children; rent was collected on Sunday. Molly Brown used her huge walking staff, decorated with flowers and ribbons, to walk up the center aisle to pew 6.

At Christmas 1979, the parish received news that Pope John Paul II had named the cathedral a minor basilica—one of twenty-nine in this country. The term is reserved for very important churches outside of Rome whose history, architecture, activities, and community service are central to the functioning of the Catholic Church. The cathedral was additionally honored when Pope John Paul II said Mass here in 1993. The church is open daily 6:00 A.M. to 6:00 P.M.; visitors are welcome. For information on building materials, see *Geology Tour of Denver's Capitol Hill Stone Buildings*.

PAINTED AND STAINED-GLASS
WINDOWS FROM BAVARIA PIERCE
THE WALLS WITH LIGHT.

17 BIDDLE REEVES HOUSE
1459 PENNSYLVANIA STREET

Architectural style: QUEEN ANNE
Built: 1889
Architect: A. MORRIS STUCKERT

This house was designed for Biddle Reeves, a prosperous mining engineer and business partner of James Clemes, whose house is on Tour Three (stop 12). It boasts Queen Anne detailing: fish-scale shingling, a turret with detailed brick coursework and eave brackets, a wrought-iron chimney support, and a carved dragon over the porch.

18 HARVEY TERRACE
1450–1460 PENNSYLVANIA STREET

Architectural style: ROMANESQUE REVIVAL
Built: 1889
Architect: WILLIAM HARVEY
Cost: $20,000

William Harvey, a bricklayer and stone contractor, probably built the facade of this foursquare terrace. It is an example of the Romanesque Revival style in a middle-class setting. Dr. and Mrs. Norman Morris bought the building in 1892 and owned it until 1946. Nathan Gart, of Gart Brothers, owned it after the Morrises. In the 1960s the Shuey Building, as it is also known, headquartered various activist groups, such as the American Friends Service Committee, the American Civil Liberties Union, and Vietnam Veterans Against the War.

19 F. H. WEISS HOUSE
1449 PENNSYLVANIA STREET

Architectural style:
NEO-JACOBEAN

Built:
1929

Architect:
UNKNOWN

Erected as a multiresidential building, this house was purchased and managed by Dr. F. H. Weiss. It has distinct gables and steep cross-gables, tall chimneys, and windows with carved stone transoms. Elaborate brickwork with stone exemplifies the Neo-Jacobean style, most common between 1890 and 1915.

1 4 4 9   P E N N S Y L V A N I A
LARGE WINDOWS WITH CARVED STONE TRANSOMS DOMINATE
THE FACADE OF THIS NEO-JACOBEAN–STYLE HOUSE.

CHARLINE PLACE
1419–1441 PENNSYLVANIA STREET

Architectural style: RICHARDSONIAN ROMANESQUE
Built: 1890
Architects: VARIAN AND STERNER

The once regal Charline Place was originally built by Charles W. Smith and named for his daughter. Henry M. Porter, Smith's brother-in-law, helped him design this mansion. It is unusual because it was originally designed as four large, connected townhouses. From the street it is not apparent that the four townhouses form a U shape, creating a narrow interior courtyard that allows light into each of the houses. In 1902 it was remodeled into twelve fancy apartments. By the time the Charline sold in the 1970s, the building had forty-two units. Construction in possibly the 1920s added terrazzo flooring and stuccoed walls. This created the now mazelike hallways connecting the many apartment units, storage areas, laundry room, and the courtyard, now hidden from view.

Note that the tower on the southeast corner of the building is visually balanced by a steep cross-gable on the north side. The conical roof of the turret echoes the shape of the steep dormers and cross-gables as well. The original design boasted a full-length, open front porch, which has now been enclosed to increase rental space, and a lovely large garden extending south to 14th Avenue, which, like many others, has given way to more apartment buildings.

On the south side of the building, elaborate wrought-iron grillwork has been installed under Romanesque-style arches on the second floor. Note the variety of building materials at the edge of the building from the street side to the alley. The facade and most of the south side are covered in rusticated stone; farther back, however, are pink brickwork and stucco covering what were originally wooden sleeping porches. The carriage house is extant but has also been stuccoed over. See *Geology Tour of Denver's Capitol Hill Stone Buildings*, part of this series, for information on the building materials.

CHARLINE PLACE, CA. 1890.

MILHEIM HOUSE
1355 PENNSYLVANIA

D&L

Architectural style: TRANSITIONAL FOURSQUARE
Built: 1893
Architect: UNKNOWN
Cost: $10,000

Now located at 1515 Race Street, the Milheim House stood across the street from the Molly Brown House for ninety-six years. In 1893, John and Mary Milheim purchased the land just prior to the Silver Crash. John, born in Switzerland, made his fortune developing scales for weighing hay wagons. He also had real estate holdings and opened the city's first bakery. John died in 1910, and Mary owned the house until her death in 1930. After she died, it successively became a boardinghouse, apartments, and offices, like many Capitol Hill mansions.

In the early 1980s an oil firm purchased the property and invested $200,000 in its restoration, but the company eventually outgrew it and sold it to the Colorado State Employees Credit Union. The credit union hoped to build a bank at the southwest corner of 14th and Pennsylvania, but their efforts were unsuccessful. They demolished an apartment house on that corner and built a parking lot instead. They also considered destroying the Milheim House, but preservation organizations opposed it. Against the credit union's wishes, the Denver Landmark Preservation Commission designated the house a landmark. The credit union then offered $40,000 to anyone who would move the house. Ralph Heronema and James Alleman accepted the offer and moved the structure, in one piece, to a vacant lot at Colfax and Race on September 15–16, 1989. It is the largest house move to date west of the Mississippi. The move averaged 1 mile an hour; trees were trimmed, power lines buried, and traffic signals temporarily relocated to accommodate it. When the house arrived by its new location, it remained in the middle of Race Street for a few weeks awaiting a foundation.

Preservationists always consider moving a building out of its original context to be a last resort. However, the new owners have done considerable work in caring for the property. They will never recoup their financial investment, although they feel the effort was well worth it.

THE MILHEIM HOUSE BEING MOVED
IN 1989. PHOTO: COURTESY OF
HISTORIC DENVER, INC.

22 EVERTS HOME
1344 PENNSYLVANIA STREET

Architectural style:
ROMANESQUE REVIVAL

Built:
1886

Architect:
WILLIAM LANG

No longer standing, the Everts Home, or Monti Mansion, was an architectural match to 1340 Pennsylvania. With its retaining wall, rough coursed stone, shingled porches, and third-floor turret, it was a graceful counterpart to the Molly Brown House next door. The house was demolished in 1966 when the American Baptist Churches of the Rocky Mountains built a modern office building. The front over-mantel was salvaged and can now be seen in the entryway at the Molly Brown House.

Joshua Monti owned a grocery store in Georgetown in its heyday. He also invested in mining, cattle ranching, and dry goods. Monti died in 1916; the Denver Museum of Natural History's gate at Colorado Boulevard and Montview was built in his memory.

23 ST. MARY'S ACADEMY BUILDING
1370 PENNSYLVANIA STREET

Architectural style: NEOCLASSICAL

Built: 1911

Architect: UNKNOWN

St. Mary's Academy, now the Pennsylvania Commons, rises gracefully at the corner of 14th and Pennsylvania. Founded on June 27, 1864, the academy opened as the premier Catholic girls' school in Colorado. In 1882, Mother Mary Pancratia Bonfils oversaw the construction of a fine new brick structure on the old St. Mary's campus at 15th and California Streets. Sister Pancratia purchased land and in 1911 opened a new home for St. Mary's, close to both the Cathedral of the Immaculate Conception and the home of Molly Brown, who was one of St. Mary's "financial angels."

When the academy moved to South University Boulevard in Cherry Hills in 1951, the F. W. Woolworth company bought this building for its offices. It changed hands again in 1968, becoming home to the Parks School of Business. It was remodeled in the 1980s for offices and condominiums and is currently the Salvation Army headquarters.

1 3 4 4

P E N N S Y L V A N I A

Photos are about all that remains
of the Lang-designed Everts Home,
seen here in 1889.

Photo: Courtesy of

Historic Denver, Inc.

GEORGE W. BALLANTINE RESIDENCE
1361 PEARL STREET

Architectural style: QUEEN ANNE
Built: CA. 1889
Architects: UNKNOWN

This house is a lone reminder of what the block might have looked like prior to the mid-twentieth century when single-family homes were pulled down for apartments. Its most prominent owner was George W. Ballantine, born in Missouri in 1848, who came to Denver for the first time with an ox team in 1859. He moved to Nebraska seven years later, and at twenty started the first lumberyard in Lincoln. Five years later he married May Sherwin. The couple had two sons. May died in 1888.

In 1877 Ballantine went to work for the Chicago Burlington & Quincy Railroad Company as a livestock agent for a short time. January 1887 found him in Denver and working as general manager for the Denver Union Stockyard Company. He remained the vice president and general manager of the company, which became a very important regional business, for twenty-eight years. Ballantine is credited with planning and holding the first stock show, starting an annual tradition now known as the National Western Stock Show.

He met and married his second wife, Ida Winne, in 1890. The house at 1361 Pearl Street was their first home. In 1903 they moved to 1450 High Street.

There are few definitive records of the residents of this house on Pearl Street until 1910. Blanche Bowen bought the house and owned it at least through the 1950s. In 1910 the house became a boardinghouse. That year's lodgers included a filmmaker and his family, a railroad bookkeeper and his family, and a railroad timekeeper. Three salesmen—one in commercial shoes, one in wholesale millinery, and one in lumber—also called the house home.

In 1893 only the west side of the street had been developed, with five residences. The Vance Kirkland Studio was built in 1910 (see stop 25). In 1936 a filling station was built next to the studio on the northwest corner of 13th and Pearl, and in the 1950s and 1960s, apartments began to appear. The Ballantine home, the first on the block to become a multifamily residence, is the only one that remains from the Victorian era.

THE GEORGE W. BALLANTINE RESIDENCE STILL RETAINS
ITS ORIGINAL ARCHITECTURAL INTEGRITY.
PHOTO BY ANNETTE VANASSE

VANCE KIRKLAND MUSEUM AND STUDIO

1311 PEARL STREET

Architectural style: ARTS AND CRAFTS

Built: 1910–1911, 1971, 1989, 1998–2002

Architects: MAURICE BISCOE AND HENRY HEWITT,

STAFFORD CLARK, MELICK & ASSOCIATES

In 1893, English artist W. Henry Read and twelve others founded the Artists' Club, which became the Denver Art Association and later the Denver Art Museum. Two years later Read opened the Students' School of Art and in 1910–1911 built 1311 Pearl Street. The studio remained the school's headquarters until 1931.

In 1929, Vance Kirkland (1904–1981) moved to Denver from Ohio and was named director of the University of Denver's Chappell School of Art. In 1932 he resigned from the university and rented the studio at 1311 Pearl to open his own art school. Twelve years later, Kirkland purchased the building, which he used as his private studio until his death in 1981.

Kirkland produced more than 1,100 works of art in his fifty-four-year career. He is recognized as one of the great modern painters of the twentieth century. His works hang in many museums and public buildings in the U.S. and Europe, including the Denver Art Museum, Vienna Museum of Modern Art, and Budapest Museum of Fine Arts.

The luminous quality of many of Kirkland's paintings comes from a technique combining oil paint with water, a unique contribution to Abstract Expressionism. Using straps hanging from the ceiling, he suspended himself horizontally over larger canvases to create his hallmark oil-and-water mixtures and dots.

The original narrow, 1,611-square-foot building was designed with north-facing skylights; the back kitchen, bathroom, and storage spaces were added in 1971. Three terra-cotta lions, produced around 1900 for the now-demolished Denver Flatiron Building, were installed per Kirkland's wishes to ensure their survival. In 1989 a second-floor room and bathroom were added on to the back of the studio. The 2002 addition of 7,933 square feet uses brick material closely matching the original building. The annex has an enclosed patio garden and exhibits the museum's twentieth-century decorative arts and Colorado collections.

THE VANCE KIRKLAND MUSEUM AND
FOUNDATION WAS ESTABLISHED IN 1996 AND
IS OPEN DURING LIMITED HOURS. ITS PURPOSE
IS TO RESEARCH, LOCATE, PHOTOGRAPH,
MAINTAIN, AND DISPLAY KIRKLAND'S
PAINTINGS AS WELL AS AN IMPORTANT
TWENTIETH-CENTURY DECORATIVE ARTS
COLLECTION AND OTHER WORK BY
NOTABLE COLORADO ARTISTS.

PHOTO: VANCE KIRKLAND MUSEUM AND FOUNDATION

TOUR TWO

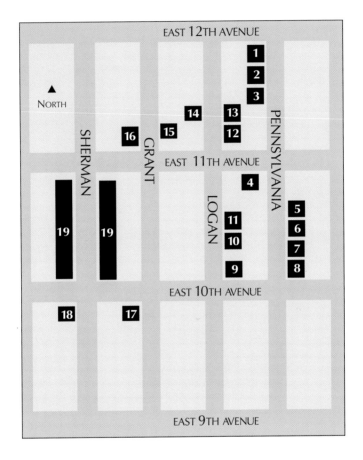

KEY

1 1165 Pennsylvania St. (Pennborough)

2 1133 Pennsylvania St. (Fleming-Hanington House)

3 1129 Pennsylvania St. (Alfred Butters House)

4 428–430 East 11th Ave. (Croke-Patterson-Campbell Mansion)

5 1066 Pennsylvania St. (Jackson House)

6 1060 Pennsylvania St. (Coe House)

7 1050 Pennsylvania St. (O'Connor House)

8 1040 Pennsylvania St. (Clark House)

9 1000 Logan St. (Brind Mansion)

10 1030 Logan St. (Stearns Mansion)

11 1034 Logan St. (Daly House)

12 1136 Logan St. (Kassler House)

13 1156 Logan St. (Helm House)

14 1159 Logan St. (Blood House)

15 1128 Grant St. (Whitehead-Peabody House)

16 1115–1121 Grant St. (Sheedy Mansion)

17 975 Grant St. (Henry M. Porter House)

18 150 East 10th Ave. (Crawford Hill Mansion)

19 1000 block of Sherman St. (Poet's Row)

1 PENNBOROUGH
1165 PENNSYLVANIA STREET

Architectural style: QUEEN ANNE
Built: 1891, 1895, 1930
Architect: UNKNOWN

The impressive Pennborough complex was originally two separate houses. The corner house was built in 1891 for Colonel David Dodge, who was instrumental in bringing the railroad to Denver. He was vice president of the Denver and Rio Grande Western Railroad and incorporated the Union Station Depot Company. The second house—the Gilluly House at 1145 Pennsylvania—was built in 1895 for another railroad man, Joseph Gilluly, a close friend of Colonel Dodge's and treasurer of the Denver and Rio Grande Western.

An annex between the two buildings went up in 1930, and by the 1940s the joined houses became the Good Samaritan Nursing Home. When the need for such homes declined, the building was renovated and converted to condominiums.

2 FLEMING-HANINGTON HOUSE   N■R D■L
1133 PENNSYLVANIA STREET

Architectural style:
NEOCLASSICAL

Built:
1893

Architect:
UNKNOWN

The Fleming-Hanington House was built in 1893, but the temple front was a style popular in the mid-1800s, so this home would have been as unusual when it was built as it is now. Josiah Fleming built the house, but it was owned by Addie Fleming-Cooper, presumed to be his daughter. Fleming was general manager of Daniels and Fisher Dry Goods until his retirement in 1898. The house was then sold to Charles Hanington, president of Mountain Motors Company, who resided here from 1914 to 1924. Hanington was a prominent civic activist and philanthropist who, at one time or another, was president of the Denver School Board, the Denver Museum of Natural History, and the Colorado Historical Society.

1 1 3 3
P E N N S Y L V A N I A
ELABORATE PORCH BRACKETS OF THE
FLEMING-HANINGTON HOUSE

ALFRED BUTTERS HOUSE

1129 PENNSYLVANIA STREET

Architectural style: QUEEN ANNE/COLONIAL REVIVAL
Built: 1890
Architect: FRANK EDBROOKE
Cost: $14,000

In addition to this residence, Edbrooke designed the Brown Palace and the Equitable Building; both are still in great condition. He gave Denver some of its first and finest commercial structures; many equally fine examples of his residential work are in this book.

Edbrooke, who had learned architecture from his English-born father, trained in Chicago. After the Chicago fire of 1871, there was plenty of rebuilding work for Edbrooke and his nine sons. Frank worked for the Union Pacific Railroad designing depots and hotels. After arriving in Denver in 1879 with commissions to build the Tabor block and the Tabor Grand Opera House, he decided to stay. Many of his early works in Denver were torn down, but the Navarre, across from the Brown Palace; the Masonic Temple at 16th and Welton; the Oxford Hotel in LoDo; the Denver Dry Building at 16th and California; and the Central Presbyterian Church at 17th and Sherman remain. Edbrooke had the largest architectural firm in Denver, and it was a training ground for many young architects. Edbrooke retired in 1915 and died in 1921. He is buried at Fairmount Cemetery in a mausoleum he designed himself.

Alfred Butters, the home's owner, was born in Maine in 1836. He was a teacher until he moved to Denver in 1860, when he became involved in the Republican Party. He was elected to the House of Representatives in 1874 and became Speaker of the House in 1876. As vice president of Colorado Savings Bank, Butters was also a prominent businessman. He sold the house in 1893 to William Russell, and it appears that they shared it for the next five years.

The house was rented to Charles Willcox, vice president and general manager of Daniels and Fisher Dry Goods, from 1908 to 1916. He commissioned the Daniels and Fisher Tower, still a major landmark on the 16th Street Mall. Willcox was known for his political alliance with Robert W. Speer, one of Denver's most controversial mayors. The house still retains its political connection as the office of Senator Ben Nighthorse Campbell.

EDBROOKE WAS INSPIRED TO USE
COLONIAL REVIVAL TOUCHES ON THIS
QUEEN ANNE STRUCTURE.

4 CROKE-PATTERSON-CAMPBELL MANSION

428–430 EAST 11TH AVENUE

Architectural style:
(FRANCIS I)
CHATEAUESQUE

Built:
1891

Architect:
ISAAC HODGSON

This spectacular mansion is a beautiful French Renaissance chateau. It is an adaptation of the architecture of the Loire Valley and was modeled after the French Chateau d'Azay-le-Rideau, built in 1520. Thomas Croke, a Wisconsin school-teacher and agriculturalist, came to Denver and made it big as a merchant. He built this mansion and sold it to Thomas Patterson, a native of County Antrim, Ireland. Patterson had immigrated to the United States in 1849, served in the Civil War, and passed the bar exam in 1867. He came to Denver in 1872. In 1890, Patterson gave up his law practice and purchased the controlling interest in the *Rocky Mountain News*. He remained interested in journalism and politics until his death in 1916. The house then passed to his daughter, Margaret, and son-in-law, Richard Crawford Campbell. The chateau has been renovated into office space, and is rumored to be haunted.

For more information about this mansion, see *Geology Tour of Denver's Capitol Hill Stone Buildings,* another book in this series.

5 JACKSON HOUSE
1066 PENNSYLVANIA STREET

Architectural style: QUEEN ANNE

Built: 1887

Architect: UNKNOWN

Very little is known about this house, built in 1887 for Ira B. Jackson. Its classic Queen Anne styling includes an asymmetrical facade with a second-story cutaway bay window. Note the steeply pitched roof, front-facing gable, and textured shingles. The etched glass on the door is a replacement.

▲

4 2 8 – 4 3 0 EAST **1 1**TH

THE TURRET OF THOMAS PATTERSON'S CHATEAUESQUE MANSION

6 COE HOUSE
1060 PENNSYLVANIA STREET

Architectural style: DENVER SQUARE
Built: 1890
Architect: UNKNOWN

This house was built for William Coe. A variety of decorative elements create interest in the facade, such as the detailed stone carving and the beautiful leaded glass windows on either side of the front door and over the larger bay window. With its deep, overhanging eaves and third-floor porch, the house has a Craftsman look despite its Queen Anne building materials.

7 O'CONNOR HOUSE
1050 PENNSYLVANIA STREET

Architectural style:
DENVER SQUARE

Built:
1899

Architects:
FISHER & FISHER

This house was built for Dr. John O'Connor, chief surgeon for the Denver and Rio Grande Western Railroad. He was most likely an acquaintance of Colonel Dodge's and Joseph Gilluly's; Dodge lived at the Pennborough complex (stop 1). The house sports a strong architectural design with Corinthian capped columns, blond brick, quoins, and symmetrical windows. Glazed brick surrounds the front door and the second-floor central windows. The leaded glass windows have a fish-scale pattern.

8 CLARK HOUSE
1040 PENNSYLVANIA STREET

Architectural style: QUEEN ANNE
Built: 1892
Architect: UNKNOWN

This home, built for Mary Clark, is unusual in Denver for its staggered, continuous wood shingling over the walls and roof. The house has a typical asymmetrical facade, with an irregular and steeply pitched roofline. The original wooden roofing has been replaced with composition roof tiles.

1050 PENNSYLVANIA
A SOPHISTICATED COMBINATION OF ARCHITECTURAL ELEMENTS

9

BRIND MANSION

1000 LOGAN STREET

Architectural style: CRAFTSMAN

Built: 1908

Architects: STERNER & WILLIAMSON

The Brind Mansion was built in 1908, after the Brinds outgrew their first house at 825 Logan (see *Geology Tour of Denver's Capitol Hill Stone Buildings*, also part of this series, for information on 825 Logan). The mansion was designed for Maria Brind, whose husband, J. Fitz Brind, owned the Butterfly-Terrible Mine and was president of Insoloid Fuse Company, which made explosives for mining. He was also a fairly well-known lithographer and oil painter, whose subjects were typically mining towns. Maria Brind, who was heavily involved in charitable activities, died in 1914. Mr. Brind stayed on in the mansion until 1919, when he sold it to Claude Staten.

Staten came to Denver from Texas and was president of Staten and Burchfield, an investment and real estate business. Shortly after his death in 1926, the house was sold to brothers Arthur and Matthew Gmeiner, both CPAs. The Gmeiners expanded the building, and the house became home to the relocated Parks School of Business. It was sold again in 1956 to architect and engineer Arthur Axtens, whose many designs include the Farmers Union Building, Colorado Woman's College, Steck Elementary, Ashley Elementary, and Epiphany Episcopal Church. The Axtenses sold the house in 1970 to Thomas Pino.

Note the elegant decorative brickwork and the numerous windows that fill the house with light. The marble steps in front and the wainscoting in the entry vestibule are made of the same marble. The house has recently undergone extensive restoration.

Sterner & Williamson used
brick, tile, and iron in this
Craftsman-style home.

10

STEARNS MANSION

1030 LOGAN STREET

Architectural style: SPANISH COLONIAL REVIVAL

Built: 1896

Architect: HARRY WENDELL

The Stearns Mansion was built in 1896 for Joel Stearns. The interior is Classical Revival. Architect Harry Wendell also designed the entrance gate lodge at Fairmount Cemetery. This turn-of-the-century, Spanish-style house is quite unusual, as the Queen Anne style was the height of fashion during the high Victorian period.

The paired chimneys on the south side are reminiscent of the missions of the Southwest. The tiled roof and extensive use of wrought iron further exemplify the Spanish influence. The house's windows show an interesting interplay of squares and arches. The wrought iron on the retaining wall and front gate is original.

President of Mountain Electric Company, the highly social Joel Stearns was listed on the social register and counted among his memberships the Denver Club, the Denver Country Club, and the University Club. He died in 1920.

THE FINEST EXAMPLE OF WROUGHT-IRON
WORK ON THIS TOUR

11 DALY HOUSE
1034 LOGAN STREET

D⬛L

Architectural style:
DENVER SQUARE/
ECLECTIC

Built:
1894

Architect:
UNKNOWN

Thomas Daly was born in Wisconsin in 1858, and like many young men of the time, ventured west to make his fortune. After working in Leadville as a miner and insurance representative, he settled in Denver in 1895 and in 1905 founded and became president of Capitol Life Insurance Company. He lived here until his death in 1921.

The house is termed "eclectic" because of its combination of elements, such as Craftsman eave brackets and wide, overhanging eaves, arched windows, and Romanesque Revival building materials with a basic Foursquare design. The three-story front porch gives the house an imposing presence. For information on the building materials, see *Geology Tour of Denver's Capitol Hill Stone Buildings.*

12 KASSLER HOUSE
1136 LOGAN STREET

Architectural style: QUEEN ANNE

Built: 1892

Architect: UNKNOWN

This lovely home was built in 1892 for Edwin Kassler. Born in 1866, Kassler was a Denver native—a rare find in his day. He remained in Denver all his life and became director of the United States National Bank and the Mountain States Telephone and Telegraph Company.

The structure is unusual for a Queen Anne because the facade is deceptively simple, similar to the Whitehead-Peabody House (stop 15), but even more stark. On the north and south sides of the house are typical Queen Anne details: a turret, rounded windows, and sandstone lintels. In 1997 the house was purchased and split into nine condominium units sporting original wood floors and simple, classically styled interior woodwork.

1 0 3 4 L O G A N
THE DEEP FRONT PORCH OF THE DALY HOUSE

13 HELM HOUSE
1156 LOGAN STREET

Architectural style: QUEEN ANNE
Built: 1886
Architect: UNKNOWN

The Helm House was built in 1886 for Judge Joseph C. Helm, who served on the Colorado Supreme Court from 1883 to 1892. All doors and windows are multipaned with their original glass. The house has original shingling; note the three styles of shingles on the porch alone.

14 BLOOD HOUSE
1159 LOGAN STREET

Architectural style:
QUEEN ANNE
Built:
1886
Architect:
UNKNOWN

J. H. Blood, a prominent Denver lawyer whose wife had come to Denver in a covered wagon as a small child, had this house built in 1886. Diminutive compared to its neighbors, the house is a classic Queen Anne. Its cutaway bay window has a wonderful carved starburst in the pediment. At the back is the original carriage house.

Take a minute to compare the facade of this house with the rather stark Kassler House (stop 12). Both structures are Queen Anne and yet very different.

1 1 5 9 L O G A N
THE SUNBURST ON THE BLOOD HOUSE

15 WHITEHEAD-PEABODY HOUSE

D L

1128 GRANT STREET

Architectural style: QUEEN ANNE

Built: 1889

Architect: FRANK E. EDBROOKE

Cost: $15,000

This house was designed for Dr. William Whitehead, a Virginian who served directly under Robert E. Lee as a surgeon during the Civil War. After the war, he moved to Denver and in 1884 was elected to the city council; he was also chairman of the Colorado Medical Society. He died in 1902.

James Peabody rented the mansion in 1903, using it as the official governor's residence for the rest of his term. Born in Vermont in 1852, Peabody moved to Cañon City, Colorado, where he served as city clerk, treasurer, and alderman; and Fremont County clerk and recorder. He was serving his second term as mayor when nominated for governor by the Republican State Convention in 1902. Governor Peabody, who was actively involved with new citizens' alliances formed to wage war against organized labor, found himself dealing with the Western Federation of Miners' strikes in Colorado's mining districts. Wanting to make Colorado a "safe place for the investment of capital," he believed domestic tranquillity should be attained at any cost. His means to prevent violence was the Colorado National Guard; confrontations with the strikers were sometimes bloody.

Mine owners and businessmen formed the Business Men's Peabody Law and Order League to help with his renomination, but his actions during the strikes nearly cost him the 1904 reelection. Labor candidate Alva Adams was nominated by the Democrats and appeared to have won by a close margin. Peabody and the Republicans contested the election. The *Rocky Mountain News* reported that "furious debates, fisticuffs and fireworks galore" resulted in a statehouse in which "legislators carried pistols strapped to their frock coats." Adams conceded defeat and Peabody was seated as governor on the condition that he resign immediately. Following the election fiasco, Governor and Mrs. Peabody returned to Cañon City. He died in November 1917.

The estate has sold many times; some people have noticed a "spooky" atmosphere here (see Phil Goodstein's *Ghosts of Denver*). For information on building materials, see *Geology Tour of Denver's Capitol Hill Stone Buildings*.

Double chimneys spring from the steep roofline of the Whitehead-Peabody House.

16

SHEEDY MANSION

D⬚L

1115–1121 GRANT STREET

Architectural style: QUEEN ANNE

Built: 1892

Architects: E. T. CARR AND WILLIAM FETH

Cost: $80,000

When Dennis Sheedy built this red brick and Colorado sandstone mansion, he spared no expense. Its drawing room had wall panels of delicate blue silk. The ceilings were decorated with cupids and flower wreaths. The main hallway, of paneled quartersawn oak, housed large double doors with beveled glass and wrought-iron panels. The reception room was finished in bird's-eye maple with walls and ceilings of silk, and the library with cherry woodwork and quartersawn red oak ceiling beams. The house has fifteen fireplaces, and the open stairway has panels of sheepskin embossed with gold leaf and nailed in brass above the wainscoting. For information on the building materials, see *Geology Tour of Denver's Capitol Hill Stone Buildings*.

The son of an Irish immigrant who settled in Iowa, Sheedy arrived in Denver in 1863 at the age of seventeen and took a job running cattle. From these meager beginnings he went on to become president of Big Horn Cattle Company in Wyoming. Upon returning to Denver in 1881 and marrying Catharine Ryan, the daughter of his boss, he explored other business options. In 1889 he took over the bankrupt Globe Smelter, which he later sold for millions to the American Smelting and Refining Company. Sheedy became manager of Denver Union Real Estate and took over the Denver Dry Goods Company in 1894. Catharine died in 1905, and Sheedy soon married young Teresa Burke.

Because of Teresa's interest in the Sisters of Saint Joseph, who had educated her in Leavenworth, Kansas, Sheedy devoted time and effort to St. Joseph's Hospital and St. Vincent's Orphanage. He was an initial investor in land for the building of the Cathedral of the Immaculate Conception.

Sheedy died in 1927. Teresa moved to 777 Logan, where she died in 1958, leaving an estate worth about $3 million. Eventually the Sheedy Mansion became the Fine Arts Building and, in 1974, an office building. If you stand before the house and face south, you will see what was once "Millionaires Row." Lost to urban renewal were dozens of spectacular turn-of-the-century mansions like this one.

The interplay of stone and brick accentuates the dozens of windows that flood the mansion with light.

17

HENRY M. PORTER HOUSE

975 GRANT STREET

Architectural style: ECLECTIC

Built: 1913

Architect: MAURICE BISCOE

The Henry M. Porter House was designed in an eclectic style: Windows are aligned symmetrically in horizontal and vertical rows, and decorative pilasters support a simple crown over the door.

Henry Porter was born in Pennsylvania in 1838 and grew up on a Missouri farm. He came to Colorado in its early days to help build the city's first telegraph lines. Porter married Laura Smith in 1870, and they moved to Denver, where he became a successful businessman and investor. Laura was the daughter of John W. Smith, who brought an irrigation system to Capitol Hill. Porter made his fortune by investing in telegraph lines, ranching, railroads, mining, and real estate; he was also vice president of Denver National Bank. He gave a significant amount of money to the Seventh-Day Adventists, who established Porter Sanitarium, now Porter Hospital.

After the Victorian period ended—roughly 1910 in Denver—buildings retained a high quality of architectural design but one with a more streamlined building aesthetic and a return to Classical Revival styles. The elegant Edwardian exterior of this house is interesting because the north side is as decorative as the front. The brickwork, with its dark, recessed mortar, causes light and shadow to play across the facade, creating pattern and visual interest in the rather simple design.

EDWARDIAN ELEGANCE

18

CRAWFORD HILL MANSION

150 EAST 10TH AVENUE

Architectural style: FRENCH RENAISSANCE REVIVAL

Built: 1906

Architects: THEODORE BOAL AND FREDERICK HARNOIS

This mansion was the focal point of Denver society for many years. Originally the house had two addresses: The front-door address was 150 East 10th, but the Hills listed their home as 969 Sherman. Sherman Street leads directly to the state capitol, and the Hills craved association with political power.

Crawford Hill graduated from Brown University in 1883 and became a partner in his father's Denver smelting business. Known as a Republican warhorse, he went on to manage the *Denver Republican*, an influential western paper. Hill also served as director of the Denver Museum of Natural History. In 1895 he married Louise Sneed, from an aristocratic Memphis family. Upon arriving in Denver, she found Hill's mother, who had created the first social registry, to be the reigning queen of local society. Louise attacked Denver's traditional lecture and chamber music events, claiming they were too somber, and began serving champagne at her luncheons and hosting Denver's longest parties and balls, complete with champagne brunch at dawn. She also established the "Sacred Thirty-Six," an elite group of Denver socialites. Although Louise was eventually acknowledged as the leader of Denver society, her mother-in-law considered her a shameless social climber. Louise and Molly Brown never hit it off either. Still, after Molly survived the 1912 sinking of the *Titanic*, the Sacred Thirty-Six held a luncheon at the Denver Country Club in honor of the "unsinkable" heroine. Crawford Hill died in 1922; Louise continued to rule the social scene until 1942. She moved to an apartment in the Brown Palace and sold the house in 1947. She died in 1955.

The mansion became the Denver Town Club, a Jewish social organization. In 1953 a swimming pool replaced the gardens. In 1989 the club disbanded and the building was sold. A classical statue of a nude woman holding lilies, which Louise had unveiled in her garden to open the social season, was sold to help pay for the house's restoration. Haddon, Morgan & Foreman, P.C., received the Colorado Historical Society's 1990 Stephen H. Hart Award for their restoration and rehabilitation of the building.

HOME OF THE SACRED THIRTY-SIX

19

POET'S ROW
1000 BLOCK OF SHERMAN STREET

Architectural style: ART DECO/ART MODERNE

Built: 1930s

Architect: CHARLES D. STRONG

Architect Charles Dunwoody Strong designed at least eight apartment buildings on this block in the recently proposed Sherman-Grant Historic District. Born in Ohio in 1895 and raised on farms in Oklahoma and Georgia, Strong served during World War I and married after returning home. His wife's tuberculosis led to their move to Denver in 1922. Strong worked for the Harry W. J. Edbrooke firm from 1923 to 1926 and started his own firm in 1927, but the Depression soon put him out of business. In 1932 he organized the Unemployed Citizens League of Denver, which supplied unemployed workers with food and necessities, sponsored classes, and coordinated relief efforts with city and state government. It was replaced by 1933 New Deal programs. By 1936, Strong was working as an architect again and headed up his own firm.

These buildings are classic examples of the innovative and stream-lined architectural styles of the 1930s. The Robert Browning (1937), the Thomas Carlyle (1936), and the James Russell Lowell (1936) all reflect the Art Deco influence, with its emphasis on vertical elements. In this case, heavy brick piers, door surrounds, and terra-cotta spandrels add verticality.

The Mark Twain (1937) and the Nathaniel Hawthorne (1938) have the streamlined Art Moderne look. Art Moderne structures are generally smooth with horizontal grooves or lines, though, unlike these, they are usually made of stucco. The Twain has contrasting brick bands between stories, rounded corners, glass brick panels, and an entry with projecting surrounds of highly glazed, dark ceramic brick.

Strong loved literature and poetry and wrote poems for pleasure. The naming of these apartments after literary figures began with his designs in 1936; perhaps the idea was his. Later, some of the older apartments—Casa Bonita (1931), now the Robert Frost, and Casa La Vista (1931), now the Louisa May Alcott—adopted literary names as well.

ONE OF THE EARLIEST OF THE POET'S
   ROW APARTMENT BUILDINGS

TOUR THREE

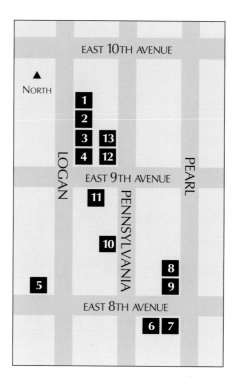

KEY

1   950 Logan St. (Campbell Mansion)
2   940 Logan St. (Allen House)
3   930 Logan St. (McNeil House)
4   900 Logan St. (Hallett House)
5   801 Logan St. (Alhambra)
6   500 East 8th Ave. (Malo Mansion)
7   777 Pearl St. (John Porter House)
8   817 Pearl St. (Olson-Kirkland Residence)
9   555 East 8th Ave. (Hart-McCourt Residence)
10 875 Pennsylvania St. (Tettemer House)
11 450 East 9th Ave. (Weckbaugh House)
12 901 Pennsylvania St. (Clemes-Lipe House)
13 945 Pennsylvania St. (Taylor House)

1 CAMPBELL MANSION

D⊞L

950 LOGAN STREET

Architectural style: GEORGIAN REVIVAL

Built: 1891

Architect: FREDERICK STERNER

Cost: $20,000

This mansion, a Georgian Revival with Classical details, was built for Frederick Thompson. In 1896, Thompson, a broker and speculator, sold this house and the one at 940 Logan to Lafayette E. Campbell, who had come to Denver to supervise the construction of Fort Logan. When Fort Logan was completed, he began supervising mines owned by David Moffat. Campbell later sold the mansion to Dr. Henry Buchtel, Colorado's governor from 1907 to 1909 as well as chancellor of the University of Denver. By 1975, before the house was renovated into office space, it had become a run-down apartment building with seventy-five tenants.

Note the prominent third-floor dormers, the carvings of whale-oil lamps, and the wonderful round front porch. On the corners of the facade, Ionic columns span the height of the first and second floors, while the porch is supported by Corinthian columns. The door, with its prominent sidelights, is characteristic of the Georgian Revival style.

2 ALLEN HOUSE

D⊞L

940 LOGAN STREET

Architectural style:
NEOCLASSICAL

Built:
1890

Architects:
VARIAN AND STERNER

One of Denver's first Neoclassical-style homes, this house has a Greek Revival front. The porches, supported by rounded Ionic columns; the low-pitched roof; and the cornice line of both the house and porch, with its wide band of trim, also reflect the Greek Revival style. The house was built in 1890 for John Allen.

The house has changed hands many times. Two of its more notable occupants were Peter McCourt, brother of Baby Doe Tabor, and Frank E. Edbrooke, noted Denver architect. Edbrooke designed the Alfred Butters House and the Whitehead-Peabody House, both on Tour Two (stops 3 and 15).

9 4 0 L O G A N
ANOTHER NEOCLASSICAL DESIGN
BY VARIAN AND STERNER

3 McNEIL HOUSE

D·L

930 LOGAN STREET

Architectural style: ECLECTIC

Built: 1890

Architects: VARIAN AND STERNER

Cost: $10,000

This fine home was built for Frederick Thompson, who later sold it to John L. McNeil, a bank executive. In 1915, McNeil sold the house to the family of Lucien Hallett, whose father lived next door at 900 Logan (stop 4). It was converted into a rooming house during the Great Depression, which is how it remained until 1974. That year, the house was restored and is once again a single-family dwelling.

The front door is difficult to see because it is recessed and slightly obscured by the round porch. The door is topped by a decorative fanlight. Upper-story shingling provides a striking contrast to the flat brickwork below.

4 HALLETT HOUSE

D·L

900 LOGAN STREET

Architectural style:
QUEEN ANNE

Built:
1888–1892

Architects:
GRABLE AND WEBER

Cost:
$28,000

This house was built for Moses Hallett. Its dominant feature is the single-story wraparound porch, now enclosed. At the third story, note the irregular, steeply pitched roof; the dormers were originally shingled. These characteristics, in combination with the massive, smooth chimneys, are reminiscent of the Shingle style. Note the interesting mix of brickwork, pillars, and sandstone carving on the second level. The home has been an apartment building since the 1940s.

Judge Hallett, originally from Ohio, was chief justice of the Colorado Territorial Court, later the state supreme court, and from 1877 to 1906, a judge for the U.S. District Court for Colorado. After retiring, he was dean of the University of Colorado Law School. Hallett also had business interests in mining, cattle, and real estate. In 1889 he sold 120 acres of land to a syndicate represented by future Denver mayor Robert W. Speer. The property was subdivided and is now known as the Arlington Park addition.

9 0 0 L O G A N
STONEWORK DETAIL

ALHAMBRA

D⊠L

801 LOGAN STREET

Architectural style: EXOTIC REVIVAL (MOORISH)

Built: 1892

Architect: UNKNOWN

Hal Sayre's Alhambra is a rare Colorado example of the Moorish Revival style. Increasing exploration and trade in the East during the late eighteenth and early nineteenth centuries spurred an interest in decorative motifs for both architecture and interiors. Exotic revivals—including Chinese, Turkish, Byzantine, Egyptian, Moorish, Mayan, and Venetian—are usually seen in theater decoration. Very few exotic revivals exist in Colorado; two notable exceptions are Denver's Mayan Theater and this house. Moorish Revival design is most often found in apartment or commercial buildings.

This yellow brick house was supposedly inspired by a trip to Spain. The house is essentially a foursquare with Moorish-style detailing. Like the Spanish Alhambra in Granada, Spain, it has ogee-inspired transom cutouts. Note the arabesque arched arcade on the three sides of the front porch. Both the interior and exterior are accented with turquoise tile. The inside of the house has cherry woodwork, and the Sayre family crest has been carved into the paneling.

Sayre was one of the first trained engineers to work in Colorado's mining camps. He specialized in mapping out claims for an interest in prospective mines, and in the process became very wealthy. He laid out the cities of Black Hawk and Central City in addition to surveying Denver. Sayre was also an officer with the Third Colorado Volunteers who rode into a village of Cheyenne and Arapaho Indians at Sand Creek on November 29, 1864. Chief Black Kettle was flying an American flag over the village to indicate they were a peaceful encampment. Colonel John M. Chivington instructed the soldiers to take no prisoners, and more than 150 Cheyenne and Arapaho men, women, and children were slaughtered. The volunteers, including Sayre, returned to Denver with Cheyenne scalps and other body parts, and these Sand Creek "trophies" were displayed at a Denver theater.

Hal Sayre died in 1926 at the age of ninety-one. His wife, Elizabeth, lived here until her death in 1937.

Ogee-inspired transom cutouts

6 MALO MANSION

500 EAST 8TH AVENUE

Architectural style:
SPANISH COLONIAL
REVIVAL

Built:
CA. 1921

Architects:
J. J. B. BENEDICT AND
HARRY MANNING

Spanish Colonial Revival architecture is most often found in Texas, Florida, Arizona, and California, where original Spanish Colonial structures exist. The Malo Mansion is the finest example of this style in Denver. Note the characteristic low-pitched clay-tile roof, balconies, stucco, and decorative ironwork. Also note the highly decorative designs under the eaves, three staggered stained-glass windows, and floral patterned columns and arches surrounding the front door; even the drainpipes are decorative. (For another Spanish Colonial Revival house, see the Stearns Mansion on Tour Two, stop 10.) The mansion was built for Edith and Oscar Malo, who worked for Edith's father, J. K. Mullen, as president of the Colorado Milling and Elevator Company.

7 JOHN PORTER HOUSE

777 PEARL STREET

Architectural style: NEO-JACOBEAN

Built: 1923

Architects: VARIAN AND VARIAN

The front of this house has beautiful red brickwork and a steep cross-gable. The north and south sides of the front porch have prominent pointed arches, and the paired chimneys are tall and ornate. Note the grouping of windows with stone window frames. The green roof tile has been used to cover the dormers. The vine-covered, attached brick porch on the south serves as an entrance to the walled garden.

The home belonged to the family of J. M. Porter, son of Henry M. Porter, whose house is featured on Tour Two (stop 17). Like his father, J. M. was a successful Denver entrepreneur and philanthropist. The house was subsequently occupied by Catholic Archbishop Urban J. Vehr, who had an intricate rose garden and a private chapel added. The home is now used as office space.

5 0 0 EAST **8**TH

THE ORNATE DOOR SURROUND OF THE ELEGANT MALO MANSION

8

OLSON-KIRKLAND RESIDENCE
817 PEARL STREET

Architectural style: FOURSQUARE

Built: 1904   Cost: $4,200

Architect: UNKNOWN

Albert Byron Olson was born in 1885, the only surviving son of Scandinavian immigrants. His father ran a dry goods store on Larimer Street and retired in 1910 at the age of sixty-five. The Olsons had moved to Denver from Montrose, Colorado, in 1904, the year of Kirkland's birth, and it was in Montrose that his mother first noticed Albert's interest in drawing. When the family moved to Denver, Albert was enrolled at Manual (Training) High School where his artwork was encouraged. After high school he studied at the Students' School of Art with Henry Read (see Tour One, stop 25). Albert continued his studies by attending the Pennsylvania Academy of Fine Arts in Philadelphia and spent a year studying works of art in Paris. After visiting more art museums in London, Madrid, and Florence, he returned to Denver.

Olson's work was highly acclaimed and sought by private collectors. In the 1930s he traveled to Capri, Italy, where he met Anne Oliphant from Beaver, Pennsylvania. They were married in 1937. Olson died in 1940 after a brief illness. Anne then married the important Colorado painter and educator Vance Kirkland, who had been a good friend of Olson's. Anne died in 1970 and Vance Kirkland continued living in the house, five blocks down the street from his studio, until his death in 1981.

The unremarkable exterior of this Foursquare home with Craftsman influences hid from the street an elegantly landscaped urban garden. The garden borrowed the view of the mansion, gardens, and fountain from the house on Ninth Avenue. The Pearl Street house had sheltering catalpa trees, massive pines, a lily pond with a small bridge, and a patio. Kirkland created a garden mural that is now shattered and broken; the Vance Kirkland Museum is restoring the piece and will reinstall it at 1311 Pearl. There were also many modern sculptures by the likes of Georges Dyens, Robert Mangold, William Joseph, Roger Kotoske, and Angelo Di Benedetto. Although the house and grounds have undergone adaptations over the years, its association with prominent Colorado artists makes this property an important Denver landmark.

THE GARDEN IN 1981, WITH LILY POND,
MURAL, AND SCULPTURES. THE HOUSE IS ON
THE LEFT. THE VIEW LOOKS SOUTH, WITH A
WALL OF THE HART-MCCOURT CARRIAGE
HOUSE AND RESIDENCE VISIBLE BEYOND
A 12 x 12–FOOT MURAL, MYSTERIES IN
MY NEBULOUS GARDEN, EXECUTED IN
1962–1963 BY VANCE KIRKLAND.
PHOTO: VANCE KIRKLAND MUSEUM AND FOUNDATION

9

HART-McCOURT RESIDENCE
555 EAST 8TH AVENUE

Architectural style: ITALIAN RENAISSANCE REVIVAL

Built: 1897–1898 Cost: $10,000

Architect: UNKNOWN

As substantial as this house is with its clean lines and balanced facade, its occupants and their ties to Denver's history are even more significant. Dr. and Mrs. Charles N. Hart moved to Denver in 1878 and built the house after their children were grown. They had three children, but only two are listed as living in this residence: Richard and Francis. Richard, a Harvard graduate, married a Denver woman, Elizabeth Jerome, who was involved with the Denver Civic Symphony, the Monday Forum, the Colonial Dames, and St. John's Social Service Committee. Elizabeth and Richard had three children, one of whom, Stephan H. Hart, inherited his father's library, famous for its biographies, which enhanced the collection of the Stephan H. Hart Library at the Colorado Historical Society.

In 1909 the first warranty deed was recorded for the new owners, the Peter McCourt family. Peter McCourt was a first-generation Irish American, one of fourteen children, born in Wisconsin in the late 1850s. His most famous sibling, Elizabeth, is best known as "Baby Doe," the second wife of Horace A. W. Tabor. Baby Doe's legend is second only to Molly Brown's in Colorado's folklore.

Tabor made millions from mining claims and investments in Colorado and built the Tabor Opera House in 1881. Peter McCourt came to Denver to act as the assistant manager and then manager of the opera house. He managed the Broadway Theater and the Tabor Theater until 1925 and 1920, respectively. McCourt was the leading theater impresario in Denver for more than forty-one years, and this home hosted many stars of the age. He owned this residence through the end of World War I and then moved on. When he passed away in 1929, services were held at Immaculate Conception, and his pallbearers read like a Who's Who of Denver; they included George W. Ballantine, Sr., the original owner of 1361 Pearl Street (see Tour One, stop 24).

SOME OF DENVER'S MOST PROMINENT
CITIZENS HAVE LIVED IN THIS HOUSE.
PHOTO BY ANNETTE VANASSE

10 TETTEMER HOUSE
875 PENNSYLVANIA STREET

Architectural style: NEOCLASSICAL

Built: 1908

Architect: UNKNOWN

J. K. Mullen built this home the same year he built the Weckbaugh House (stop 8). A Neoclassical with a full-height entry porch and Ionic columns, it was shared by two of his daughters, Edith and May, until Edith married and moved to the Malo Mansion (stop 6). Mullen lived at 896 Pennsylvania, while Katherine, his fourth daughter, lived at 860 Pennsylvania. Unfortunately, both houses were demolished.

11 WECKBAUGH HOUSE
450 EAST 9TH AVENUE

Architectural style:
FRENCH ECLECTIC

Built:
1908

Architect:
UNKNOWN

A wrought-iron fence borders the sophisticated Weckbaugh House, built by John Kernan Mullen for his daughter, Ella. The stuccoed walls and decorative panels are reminiscent of the Malo Mansion (stop 6). Prominent dormers, wrought iron, and stained glass add visual interest. On the east side of the house, note the roofline and copper vestibule on the second-floor balcony.

J. K. Mullen, born in Ballinasloe, County Galway, Ireland, immigrated to the United States with his family in 1856 to flee the potato famine. The family settled in Denver by way of Illinois and Kansas. At the age of fourteen, Mullen apprenticed with a flour miller. Eventually he saved enough money to lease and then buy the Star Mill, turning it into the multimillion-dollar Colorado Milling and Elevator Company, with 800 employees and ninety-one mills, elevators, and warehouses.

Mullen, a devout Catholic, became a legendary philanthropist. It is estimated that he gave more than $2 million to the Catholic Church. He also persuaded J. J. Brown, Dennis Sheedy, John F. Campion, and John C. Mitchell to help with the construction of the Cathedral of the Immaculate Conception. J. K. and Catherine Smith Mullen had five daughters, four of whom lived to adulthood.

Noel, Thomas J. *Colorado Catholicism and the Archdiocese of Denver,*
1857–1989. Niwot: University Press of Colorado, 1989.

Noel, Thomas J. *Denver Landmarks and Historic Districts: A Pictorial Guide.*
Niwot: University Press of Colorado, 1996.

Noel, Thomas J. *Denver's Larimer Street.* Denver: Historic Denver, Inc., 1981.

Noel, Thomas J., and Barbara S. Norgren. *Denver: The City Beautiful.*
Denver: Historic Denver, Inc., 1987.

Pearce, Sarah J., and Merrill A. Wilson. *A Guide to Colorado Architecture.*
Denver: Colorado Historical Society, 1983.

Poppeliers, John C., S. Allen Chambers, Jr., and Nancy B. Schwartz.
What Style Is It? Washington, D.C.: The Preservation Press, 1983.

Saint John's Cathedral. Denver: The Women of St. John's Cathedral, 1979.

Whiffen, Marcus. *American Architecture Since 1780: A Guide to the Styles.*
Amherst, Mass.: M.I.T. Press, 1969.

Widmann, Nancy L. Cuthbert-Dines-Starkey Mansion: A History.
Denver, 1997.

Widmann, Nancy L. East Seventh Avenue Historic District: An
Application for Historic Designation. Denver, 1992.

Widmann, Nancy L. Sherman-Grant Historic District: An Application
for Landmark Designation. Denver, 1997.

Wilk, Diane. *A Guide to Denver's Architectural Styles and Terms.* Denver:
Historic Denver, Inc., and Denver Museum of Natural History, 1995.

Wilk, Diane. *The Wyman Historic District.* Denver: Historic Denver, Inc.,
and Denver Museum of Natural History, 1995.

Biographical Index